Comets and Asteroids

Space Rocks

By Greg Roza

Gareth Stevens
Publishing

Please visit our Web site, www.garethstevens.com. For a free color catalog of all our high-quality books, call toll free 1-800-542-2595 or fax 1-877-542-2596.

Library of Congress Cataloging-in-Publication Data

Roza, Greg.
Comets and asteroids : space rocks / Greg Roza.
    p. cm. — (Our solar system)
Includes index.
ISBN 978-1-4339-3816-0 (pbk.)
ISBN 978-1-4339-3817-7 (6 pack)
ISBN 978-1-4339-3815-3 (lib. bdg.)
1. Comets—Juvenile literature. 2. Asteroids—Juvenile literature. 3. Solar system—Juvenile literature. I. Title.
QB721.5.R69 2011
523.6—dc22
                                        2010013689
First Edition

Published in 2011 by
Gareth Stevens Publishing
111 East 14th Street, Suite 349
New York, NY 10003

Designer: Daniel Hosek
Editor: Greg Roza

Photo credits: Cover (top), p. 1 (top), back cover (top) © Photodisc; cover (bottom), p. 1 (bottom), back cover (bottom) © iStockphoto.com; p. 5 (top) © Digital Vision; pp. 5 (bottom), 15 (bottom right) NASA; p. 7 Johns Hopkins University Applied Physics Laboratory/Southwest Research Institute; pp. 9, 19 Shutterstock.com; pp. 13, 21 Getty Images; p. 15 (top left) ISAS/JAXA; p. 15 (top right) NASA/JPL; p. 15 (bottom left) NASA/JPL/JHUAPL; p. 17 International Astronomical Union.

Printed in the United States of America

CPSIA compliance information: Batch #CS10GS: For further information contact Gareth Stevens, New York, New York at 1-800-542-2595.

Contents

Boldface words appear in the glossary.

Space Rocks

Our **solar system** has many planets and moons. It also has many smaller objects called comets and asteroids.

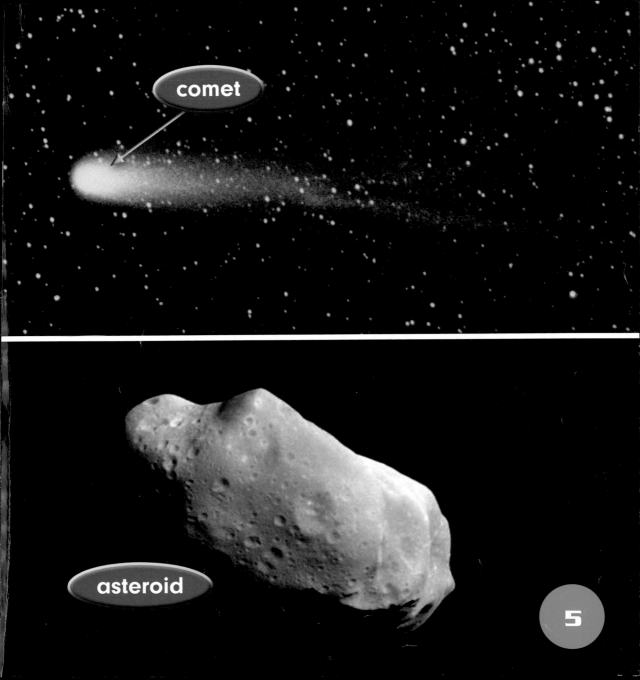

comet

asteroid

5

Dirty Snowballs

Comets form far away, outside the solar system. They are made mostly of ice and dust. Sometimes comets are called "dirty snowballs"!

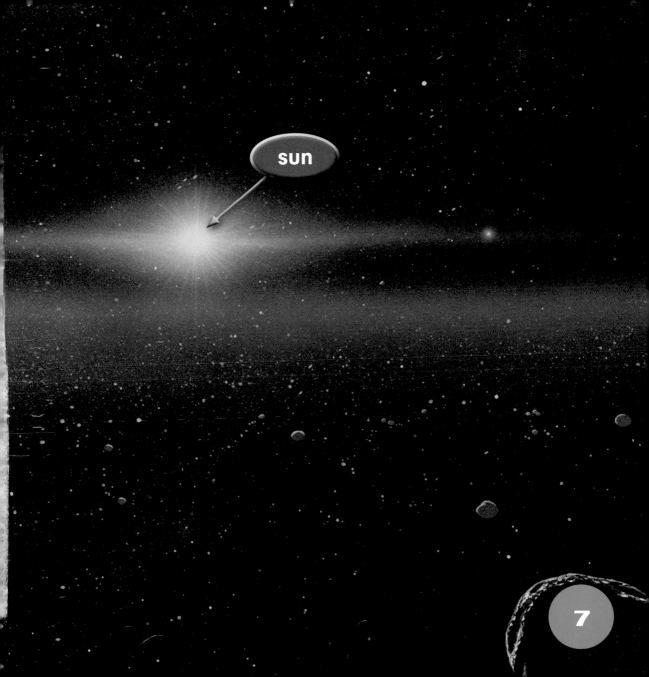

sun

7

Some comets enter the solar system. They pass close to the sun and then leave the solar system. This takes many years.

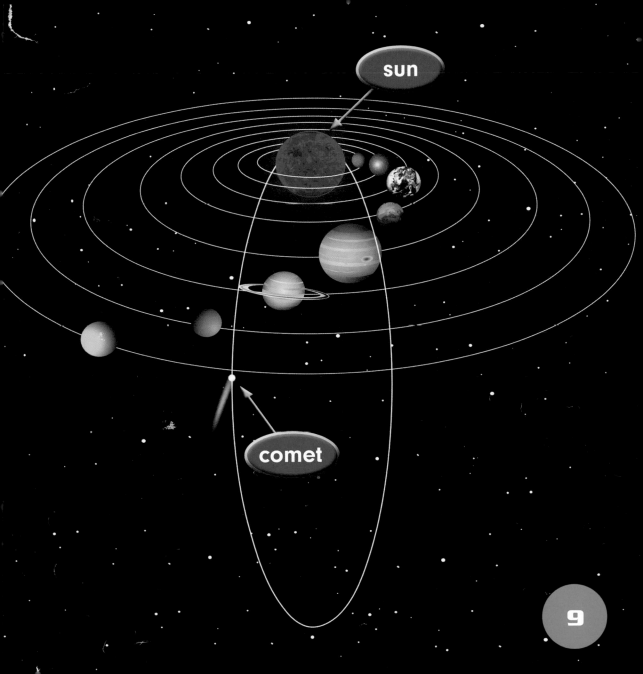

The sun's **energy** melts some of a comet's ice. The energy also blows dust away from the comet. The dust makes the comet look like it has a tail.

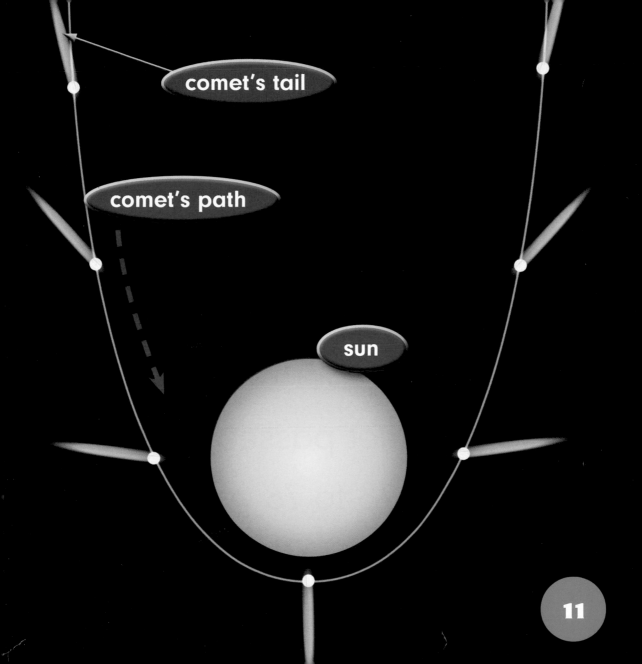

comet's tail

comet's path

sun

11

Here Comes Halley!

Some comets pass through the solar system and never return. Others return over and over. Halley's comet passes Earth once every 75 to 76 years.

Halley's comet

Let's Rock!

Asteroids are rocks left over from when the solar system formed. Some are many miles across. Others are as small as grains of sand.

Most asteroids **orbit** the sun in the space between Mars and Jupiter. This area is called the asteroid belt. It has **millions** of asteroids!

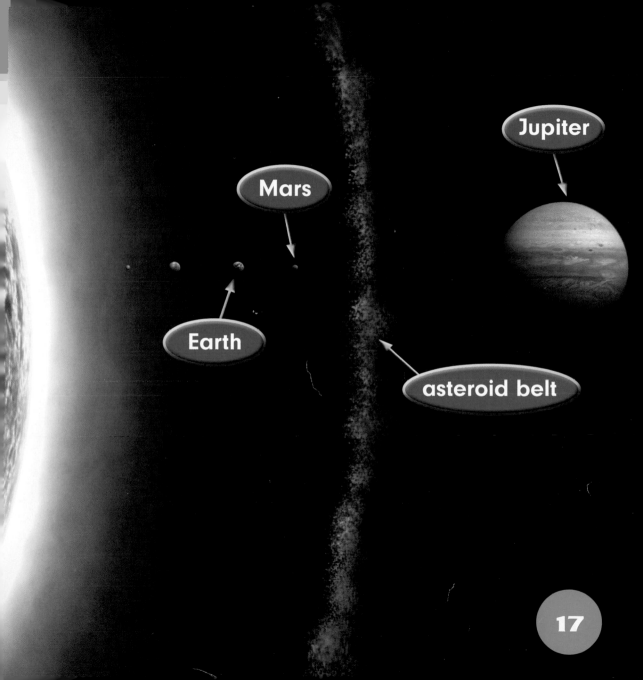

Some asteroids come close to Earth's orbit. They are called near-Earth asteroids, or NEAs. Some NEAs have even crashed into Earth!

19

Eros

In 2000, scientists sent a **probe** to study an NEA called Eros. The probe took close-up pictures of the asteroid. It also became the first probe to land on an asteroid!

probe

Eros

21

Glossary

energy: power

million: a 1,000 thousands, or 1,000,000

orbit: to travel in a circle or oval around something

probe: an unmanned spaceship

solar system: the sun and all the space objects that orbit it, including the planets and their moons

For More Information

Books

Chrismer, Melanie. *Comets*. New York, NY: Children's Press, 2008.

Kortenkamp, Steve. *Asteroids, Comets, and Meteorites*. Mankato, MN: Capstone Press, 2008.

Web Sites

Asteroids

www.kidsastronomy.com/asteroid.htm

Learn about asteroids, including the largest ones in our solar system.

Comets

www.kidsastronomy.com/comets.htm

Read about comets and see pictures of them.

Index

About the Author

Greg Roza has written and edited educational materials for young readers for the past ten years. He has a master's degree in English from the State University of New York at Fredonia. Roza has long had an interest in scientific topics and spends much of his spare time reading about the cosmos.